INSPIRED POETRY

SYLVIA BLYTH

Order this book online at www.trafford.com
or email orders@trafford.com

Most Trafford titles are also available at major online book retailers.

Print information available on the last page.

ISBN: 978-1-4120-9349-1 (sc)
ISBN: 978-1-4907-8207-2 (hc)

Trafford rev. 05/12/2017

 www.trafford.com

North America & international
toll-free: 1 888 232 4444 (USA & Canada)
fax: 812 355 4082

A Friend In Need

I walked for hours along the cliff,
I stopped, then walked some more.
You saw me on the small cliff path.
I saw you on the shore.

We stood and waved, and waved again.
I joined you on the sand.
In your eye that cry for help.
I reached and took your hand.

You said you thought I wouldn't come,
I said that I'd always try.
You didn't think that I'd care that much.
A tear was in your eye.

I told you, don't give up so soon
Your kind are much too rare,
You nearly tried to end it all.
You thought I did not care.

Your note had said you just went out,
But had not said which way.
You were not fit to go for walks
Out in that wind swept bay.

The sky was dark, the wind was cold
And blowing like a gale
You walked for miles without a coat.
Your face was very pale.

We stopped and saw the gulls in flight,
And they swooped down to the sea.
I said it's getting very cold,
Come back home with me.

We turned and looked across the sea,
And across the beach so bare.
You turned and whispered in my ear,
"I didn't think you'd care".

I said I saw you on the beach,
Maybe you saw me too.
And if you'll not give up on me,
I'll not give up on you.

We went back and lit the stove.
And made a pot of tea.
And talked and laughed into the night.
My lifelong friend and me.

© Sylvia. B. Blyth.14.2.1989.

A Natter with Nella

I had a natter with Nella

When out with my friends today.

It was the first time we'd spoken for quite a long time

And boy, what a lot we had to say.

We spoke of some people around us

Who we hadn't expected to see

We spoke of the things that surrounded us

Things that she liked and were amusing to me.

We had such a lovely natter,

Of everyday things-and the rest.

Catching up on life with the friends you have missed

Is one of lifes things I like best.

A friend's going missing this Summer

She said she would be gone for some weeks.

I expect the phone will be red hot when she returns

And we'll be chatting about her visit to the Peaks.

© Sylvia. B. Blyth 22.07.2012

SEAFARERS SECRET

Sailing calmly with the breeze,
And oft' I have sailed before,
Sailing 'neath the dipping sun,
And headed for the shore.

We saw the fishing boats set off,
To catch the outward tide,
I wondered if the crew with me
Shared what I felt inside.

No one spoke of any thoughts,
Of panic or unease.
They simply carried on their work
And sailed on in the breeze.

We had thought to sail in,
And anchor in the bay.
But something barred our entering
'Till we drifted right away.

The Crew said "Never worry,
We'll catch the morning tide",
But something seemed to pull us back
To face the Ocean wide.

We tried to be as 'big brave men',
As we sat and ate one night.
Then. "Come on board", the first mate said,
"I see a strange big light".

The light was right above us
As we stood on deck in awe,
We left our food the way it was,
And closed the cabin door.

We stood transfixed and staring,
We saw a silver dome,
"I don't like this" the first mate said,
"Can we not go home?"

The dome had started spinning,
But we still stood there transfixed,
We stood in awe yet terrified
Now the feelings there were mixed.

Then, all at once, each one of us,
Was lifted off the deck.
The light was now around us,
An eerie, strange effect.

The dome was taking over,
The light was everywhere,
Some creatures stood around us
As we hurtled through the air.

All that took place so long ago,
Who could believe our plight,
Who could believe a silver craft
Could steal us in the night.

We could not tell a single soul,
And neither could we rest.
We could not find our ship again
Our dear Marie Celeste.

EPILOGUE

If you ever see her,
When sailing out one day.
Never try to board her,
Just send her on her way.

But just before you sail away
Throw flowers pure white,
And a little prayer for the gentlemen there
Who disappeared that night.

© Sylvia B Blyth 8 July 1996.

A Senior Day

Where did I leave my shopping bag
My walking stick and brolly?
If I cannot find it
I'll have to use my trolley.

But, I really need my shopping bag
With all my junk down in it.
My keys and letters and my purse,
That I'll need at any minute.

I really need my biro,
I use it quite a lot,
And, also there's my glasses
I nearly them forgot.

I really need my shopping bag
I take it everywhere,
Oh dear, now I remember-
It's down behind my chair.

A-MORAL

People went about their work
On a bright and peaceful day.
Then someone with a grudge and a gun,
Came and blew a man away.

It wasn't even wartime
Or even gangland feud,
Or even a bad word overheard,
And the whole lot misconstrued.

It may have been a jealousy,
And a whole town fell apart,
What the cause, who can tell,
But, someone's shot right through the heart.

Someone walking home alone,
No cash to catch a bus,
Then the rape at knifepoint,
"Don't dare to make a fuss!!"

Knives are used for hobbies
With a fork we use a knife,
A knife we use for cutting cheese,
But, whose blade took the life

Someone with a problem?
Someone sick with rage?
Someone wild and all tied up
Like a tiger in a cage?

It's the brain behind the trigger,
It's the brain behind the blade.
The brain behind the evil deed,
That's where the blame is laid.

Someone's life's not perfect?
Something just not right?
Someone's stopped by a bullet or a knife,
And they're heading for the light.

That little light out yonder,
The one they speak about.
The one you reach when you're all washed up,
And your own body's light's gone out.

There's a moral to this story,
Concerning gun or knife,
When taken up in anger,
They threaten every life.

© Sylvia. B. Blyth 4.7.96.

ACROSS THE MOOR

Across the moor and in the vale,
Here it holds a happy tale,
Friends for life, - that's friends for ever,
Living near the gorse and heather.

Seeing through the mist at dawn,
Cattle, chickens, the sheep and the fawn,
Seeing the sunrise over the hill,
A place to feel happy and it always will.

Watching at springtime, crocus on the lawn,
Lambs hopping round mother, newly born,
Seeing fresh daffodils, bright yellow and cream,
Iris so delicate down by the stream.

Birds in the morning, hear how they sing,
Birds making nests and birds on the wing,
The bees and the butterflies hover round flowers,
Life in the garden, - watch it for hours.

©Sylvia B Blyth 7.2.2012

ALL CHANGE

My name is Pat Sullivan and I work for the family laundry. My brother Harry and I share the driving of one of the delivery vans. Snow had been falling on the night of December the 4th and Harry was driving as it was his turn. That day was my day for loading and unloading laundry and sorting paper work. We work like this on alternate days. We had only been on the move ten minutes when I felt the skid and the jerk on my safety strap brought me out of my deep reverie. I had been thinking how I wished this was the end of the day instead of the beginning. Snow covered everything and we had a problem coming to a halt slithering sideways. It was just 7.45am and still quite dark as Harry got out to see what was outside the van. When he returned he put his head near the part opened window "It was a dog. It ran out in front of us." he said. "Well, where is it now?" I asked peering through the caked up windscreen. I turned on the wipers again to get a better view. "There it is," I pointed to a light brown bundle crouched by the roadside. We both went to see if it was O.K. He was alright, just a bit shocked as we were. He was wearing a lead and I picked up the end of it. He got up and started to pull me along the side of the field which was on our left. He kept on pulling until I followed him alongside of the field to a railway line. I looked down the line some hundred and fifty yards and in the dim light I saw the roof of the station. In the station was a train but it was at an awkward angle. As we got nearer to the station we saw the carriages half on the platform. They were tipped up causing the roof of the carriages to touch the opposite side of the platform roof. I turned round to shout to Harry. Luckily he wasn't too far behind me. He caught up and saw the wrecked train. We had seen no other people around. We had a quick look at the train but couldn't do anything as it was in such a difficult position. We went back to the van with the dog and drove to the station car park. There was still no one around, so Harry phoned on his mobile to get the emergency services. While we were waiting, we heard some groaning and someone calling from the first carriage. We couldn't see them so we called out to them that someone was on the way to help. "Harry, I recognised that voice," I said," I think that sounds like Sidney from next door." "Is that you Sid?" I called up to the train, are you hurt?" "I think me legs 'ave gorn." said Sid. There was quiet for a little while, then Sid called out "Have you seen anything of a ginger dog?" Harry called out "Yes we have got him, he led us to the train. And by the way what is his name?" "His name is Sandy. Is that you two from next door? We must stop meeting like this." Then Harry laughed and said that he wouldn't make it a habit. Then Sid said "Will you do something for me Pat? I want you to phone the Mayor's house to tell his wife to come to the station as there has been an accident. We should have been home at dinner time yesterday and he is sitting beside me here. I don't think he is badly hurt but he got knocked out when we tipped over. We've been to the Bowls match in Liverpool at the weekend so we got the night train back." They all heard the sirens of the services as they pulled into the station. Firemen came running in onto the platform and quickly surveyed the situation. Within minutes there was a big hubbub of Police, Fire, and Ambulance men working out how to get the injured people out of the train. Luckily, only two Ambulances were needed. The train driver was concussed and had a broken arm. He was taken off to hospital with the others. We arranged to take the dog home with us when we had delivered our first load of laundry. As we came away from the station we saw the two local newspaper men taking pictures of Sid on a stretcher and the Mayor standing beside him holding up a big silver trophy. When our day was finished we went home and made a bed up for Sandy the dog on the landing and he settled down for the night. Next morning as I picked up the newspaper off the mat and saw a picture of Sid and the Mayor with the trophy and the story of the crash on the front page.

© Sylvia B Blyth

ALL IN THE MIND

If I could choose the perfect place
To grow my favourite flowers,
I'd do my best to make it bright
And sit for hours and hours.

Lovely greens and lovely blues
The ferns like velvet made,
Shocking pinks and lilac hues,
And sunflowers that never fade.

I'd also make a lovely lake,
Put reeds where sun will shine.
With ducks and pigeons, fish and swans,
The place would be divine.

I'd have to plant some silver birch,
The oaks and cedar too.
Lots to do and lots to dream,
All in my mental view.

An Ode for 2013 © Sylvia. B. Blyth. 2.01.2013

Here is an ode for the start of the year.
I've had a few bad moments, but still I am here.
I've seen part of the family and that was so good,
And penned a few verses, when I could.

That was the past year, twelve months gone so fast.
I start to recall some odes from the past.
I need to find concentration, must do better.
Try I must to remember, letter for letter.

The day past quite easily for THE END OF THE WORLD.
Quite a surprise for some, nothing unfurled.
Much too much rain is what we might curse,
But, pretty ole snow, could be worse, much worse.

Thank you to God for what we endure.
Help us help the sick, find them a cure.
Help us be thankful for the things we have got.
Help us look after the ones who have not.

At the end of the day and you feel you can't win,
Your dinner's "gone off" and is dumped in the bin.
Think of the poor ones outside with a fever,
They had no food yesterday, none today either.

ANDREA

What a lovely girl is she.
She walks the highways of her dreams,
She rides the horses, strong and tall,
And leads them into cooling streams.

Taken in the midst of life,
Sick of body – tired and sad.
Loved by family and friends
With memory of the life she had.

As family so close live on,
They will recall each happy day
The things they did together then,
They'll not forget her, come what may.

Time may go so fast, or slow,
But, we will find our special place.
To ones who left, we said goodbye,
But later cherish face to face.

ANGEL

Angels live in heaven,
They come down here at will.
We've got one here in Mitcham,
Who sits down at the till.

Sometimes when Jim's shopping,
He'll join up on a queue,
Sometimes there'll be another girl
Then sometimes there'll be you.

We thank you all, each lady,
We love your friendly ways,
I'm thankful for your friendly thoughts,
On all these shopping days.

ANYTHING

Give me once more the soft breeze that blows,
Let me once more hear the brook that sings.
Let me once more hear the autumn leaves fall,
Please, maybe to hear just one of these things.

Give me once more that sweet smell of corn,
Let me once more hear the birds in the trees.
Let me once more feel the sun in the morn,
Please, maybe hear the buzz of the bees.

If I could hear just one of these, though not to see,
If I could just smell the sweet flowers of spring,
Let me once more feel the bark of a tree,
I shall be grateful for any small thing.

If one day, by chance, I could see,
See the things I always hold dear,
If one day I see the leaves that fall,
Then I shall know the healer was here.

AUTUMN JOURNEY

Though they went on their way
With the Autumn Leaves falling,
Though you shed another tear
As you wake every morning.

Be sure in your heart
That the pain you may hide
Is known by your loved one
Who is still by your side.

For they didn't go far
Just through a light cloud
Then a short readjustment
To return bright and proud.

AUTUMN RAIN

The summer's going right away.
The rain is getting colder.
Squirrels are about and hunting for food
And getting so much bolder.

The sky is blue still, well now and then,
Between grey clouds of thunder,
It's time to get the brollies out.
And keeping dry there, under.

The birds are staying in the trees,
When the rain comes pouring down,
Then the thunder starts, the lightening too
And the people rush back from the town.

But, not all people will rush indoors,
Away from autumn weather,
That's okay for them but I'll get my rug
And be warm with the sides pulled close together.

BECAUSE

Because I'm much too low to reach
Because I have a slury speech
Because I cannot walk too well
And if I'm hurt I cannot yell,
Some think I'm mad or drink a lot,
They think I'm stupid, - I am not.

It's just that one time long ago
I had an awful crash.
My limbs were damaged and my brain,
But now some think I'm trash.

I got myself together,
I sorted out my life.
Now I see that they are sick
So cannot see my strife

© Sylvia Blyth. 2003.

BETRAYED

Another land, another war,
Another reason dying for.
Another leader filled with hate,
Thousands meet an awful fate.

One man with a power strong,
Enough to drag a state along.
Enough to do his bidding there,
For people's souls, he does not care.

The leader stands there oh so smart,
Uniformed to play the part,
A smile to show the world he's sweet,
And mocking dead men at his feet.

He'll stand there looking oh so smug
Like preying mantis with a bug.
He'll stand and say things just to psych,
Then like the mantis he will strike.

Little boys still fresh from school
Thin and hungry, made a fool,
Made to fight and cut to pieces,
A thousand souls the war releases.

BIG BOYS CAN CRY

Don't be afraid to cry a bit,
Isn't that what tears are for?,
For many things were just not right,
Behind our own front door.

Life could be complicated
Feelings were muddled too
Life got mad and life got sad
And fraught for me and you.

It never will be easy,
To explain why things went wrong,
Life never goes in one straight line,
Whether life be short or long.

I'll simply say I'm sorry,
That things got out of hand,
But I, like you, was unprepared,
For the shocks - you understand!.

We're all on earth for learning,
But all at varied speeds,
So please forgive me for my lapse,
In knowing all your needs.

There are many things to put behind us
Yet too many things not said or done.
There are things I needed said as a mother,
There were things you needed to hear as a son.

Too many things un-mended
Too little freedom from the start
There were times then, too when love was meant for you
But someone kept pulling us apart.

There were too many times in the night time
When you cried into your pillow on your own,
I'd have been there right away, hold your hand and I would stay,
I'd have been there if only I had known.

BIKER 2

I used to have a Motor Bike
It was a damned good goer,
But then the old back wheel fell off
Now it goes much slower.

It got me down to Brighton,
It got me to Southend,
But since my lovely tank blew up
It sends me round the bend.

Biker

There is a big, BIG motor bike,
It's owned by Dusty Miller.
But this one's sort of different,
Cause this one's got a TILLER.

It's also got a big, BIG sail,
For when the wind is strong,
Now when the wind is a whippin' up
It helps the lad along.

Way back when he ordered it,
He didn't know they'd send,
A bike with sail and tiller
To help him round the bend.

I saw him ridin' out one day,
That sail was flapping mad.
He said it saved his petrol.
For that he's very glad.

BIRD'S VISIT

That tomato picking birdie
I see she's here again,
She scouts the garden every day
Her dinner to obtain.

You might see her on the wall
Walking to and fro,
But just try not to startle her
When you turn to go.

Though she is a wild bird,
She's getting very tame.
The pigeons, when they drop- in
They are just the same.

Talk to them quite softly,
Quietly and calm
They'll get to know you gradually
And, that you'll do no harm.

I can see her, feet away
In the corner of my eye
But, if I forget and move too fast
She's off into the sky.

She's getting very cheeky
With my tomato pot,
Sometimes she tips it over
I think she'd take the lot.

BITTER SWEET

When I was very, very young
Before I knew the price of bread.
We went to get some sweets and things
Yet men had fallen - some were dead.

The war was really over then,
Some soldiers home to crying wives.
Some came home to bricks and mortar,
And nothing else to fill their lives.

Soldiers home so ill and broken,
I was too young to understand.
Not knowing too that for some others,
Were still locked in another's land.

Many more I would discover,
Home in body, but not in mind.
Others fit and fair of body,
But for them, completely blind.

When I was young, so very young
Not even old enough for school,
I didn't know the way some humans,
Were so very, very cruel.

The war machine and people dying,
Often hidden from the young,
'Til growing up and truth is unfurled,
Like flying flags and the war songs sung.

Men and women in the forces,
Some come home and some will fall.
They do their job with so much courage,
If only they didn't need to go at all.

When it's time and I am going,
With the Angel at my door,
Maybe I'll ask and maybe they'll tell me,
Will there be an end to war?

Bonds of Friends

I shed a little tear last week,
It fell into my tea,
The reason was those special friends,
Who mean so much to me.

Born so very far apart,
Away in different lands,
But, none the less we share a bond,
And trust in God's good hands.

We share the bonds of sadness,
We share the bonds of joy,
We know they're safe and happy now,
The grown up girl and boy.

I said a prayer for my good friends
And yes, I must confess
I shed a tear again today,
My tear of happiness.

BOSNIA JUST ONE SOLDIER

I should be in there somewhere,
Yet I'm floating high above.
My limbs are not obeying me
And I'm flying like a dove.

I cannot feel the bullet
That hit me in the back.
I do not know the moment
Of the enemy attack.

I'm thinking of my childhood
When I played out in the street.
And when my Mother called me in,
She said "It's time to eat."

I recall how Mother,
Would spend hours baking bread.
Would put a loaf for us to eat,
And, simply nod her head.

I recall much later times,
Of when I went to sea.
I wrote to my parents,
They wrote back to me.

Now I'm here, back home again.
But now a different war.
There's fighting in the streets now
Against the folk next door.

I think I must be dreaming,
I keep on drifting off.
I haven't breathed in lately
The air feels strangely soft.

I can see me lying there,
Sprawled out on the ground.
I don't think I'll be getting up,
I'll be dead when I am found.

A woman standing near me,
Holds a cloth that's edged with lace.
She's kneeling now, in all the mud,
To cover up my face.

For me the war is over,
What is done is done.
A war that is so hopeless
Is never ever won.

Quicker now, there must be truce,
Or all of us be killed.
When will sense step in here
And all the guns be stilled?

Two weeks my body's lain there
And, no one else's moved
Lots of dead and injured
What has this fighting proved?

BUNGEE

I will NOT do a bungee
No matter what you say,
Bouncing around on a rubber band
Is not my kind of day.

I know when people do it,
They say it's "so much fun".
But I won't bounce a single once,
So, babe I'm not the one.

So, you can keep your footie bindings
Or your high up perch,
I always scare up in the air,
Never mind the sudden lurch.

So, keep your bungee jumping
It's simply not for me.
I'd rather view from a safer pew,
That's where I will be.

BUTTERFLIES

Walking in the countryside
I saw a scene so bright.
A bush so full of butterflies
And even more in flight.

The colours were so beautiful
With black and white ones too.
Then orange and the lemon ones,
The crimson and the blue.

It all was such a splendid sight.
I stood there quite transfixed
Sometimes all the pastel tones,
And then they all were mixed.

A super big kaleidoscope,
Stole my mind that day.
The colours took me by surprise
What more can I say!

CALM AFTER THE STORM

There is, somewhere, by the sea,
To rest then wander, and rest again,
To look to one side to the foaming sea,
Then look to the other side to the rolling plain.

A sea that's steel blue in the rain,
Then sparkling aqua in the sun,
With gulls that dive and screech and squeak,
And swoop before you when the day is done.

Not far off from your seaside path,
Are field upon field of uncut corn,
Ready to harvest not far off,
And all stacked up one late summers dawn.

But not yet, still more to do,
Still pen in hand to round off the page.
Still not calm to find the words,
Because of life's turmoil and inner rage.

"Be calm", they tell me, "What's gone before,
Long years ago, and cannot be undone."
But, I know this quite well, it was me there,
Oh, I know this and survived, so for that, I won.

I got through a life, as many do,
Things unexpected, of terror and pain,
You get up and live and hide all the bad,
But, sometimes, later on surfaces again.

It's all very well to be calm and be strong,
When all's bottled up and corked like a wine.
And it's all of your battles to do what is right,
At the end of the day, the fight was all mine.

I cried and I panicked about what to do.
I cried in my pillow, like you, like you.
There was no choice, no other road to take,
Just one option open, one must do what one must do.

CARDBOARD BOX

When all the lamps are lighted
And all the streets are bare,
Does anyone notice the cardboard box,
And the man asleep in there.

Did anyone notice a cardboard box,
With the man who looked so sad.
Can anyone tell me if he's still in there
As I'm looking for my Dad.

He went away last Easter
When my parents had a row.
Dad got unhappy when he lost his job,
But we want him back right now.

I found the box - it had his name,
It was leant against some doors.
ON IT READ, Don't need it now - I'm going home-
Take the box - it's yours.

CATWALK

You used to be a boxer
Ducking and diving in the ring
Now you tread the catwalk
A rather different thing.

You've had your day as a homeless
Sleeping on the street,
But now life's looking rosey
As you've landed on your feet.

It's good to see how life can change
And someone gets a lift.
One time good then down and out,
Then comes a golden gift.

CHRISTMAS CAKE

We went down to Bognor,
For a five day Christmas break.
The dinners were fine, the coffees too,
But where's my Christmas Cake?

We had our break at Butlins.
Well earned days indeed.
They had a lovely Christmas Tree,
But where's the cake I need?

All the hall was very bright.
The décor was so nice.
The moose I tasted was just great,
But cake- there was no slice.

I know I must'nt eat too much,
But it was our Christmas break.
We had a pleasant time away
But, where's my Christmas Cake?

CHRISTMAS

Good wishes sent and presents bought,
Christ's own birthday story taught.

Candles flicker, festooned trees,
People praying on their knees.

Around a tree - the choir singing,
In the Church - the bells are ringing.

Christmas songs throughout the land,
Outstretched is the homeless hand.

Christmas joy and Christmas gladness,
But, comes to some a Christmas sadness.

People living in the street,
Without some shoes upon their feet.

People crouch in big shop doorways,
Living rough, against life's - law ways.

In the Hospice, the sad are calling
White and chill, the snow is falling.

Stories short- or stories old,
About the birth, are once more told.

Those departing at God's will,
That's life's sad and bitter pill,

Taken - in the Christmas season,
Which seems at first to have no reason.

But still we live to celebrate,
And link with those in Spirit State.

So come along and feel the glory
Remember too - The Christmas Story.

Told a thousand times before,
And will be told a thousand more.

Join celebrations for our Lord,
To send our love with one accord.

Climbing Mountains

Believe it or not, everyone has a mountain. Whether they accept it or not, is for their own judgment. This mountain I speak of is a symbol of Life and Spirit Progress.

If we wish to progress, we must live this life in the best way we know, plus knowing that when we fail in some areas, we must accept that failure is all part of our learning process and experience. It is useless to try to cover up failure. Knowing one's self is to know each little failing, however trivial it may seem. If not faced and accepted, the smallest of failures, misdeeds or ill feeling towards others who bother us, can soon become a torment in the very depths of our minds. These torments will be a block to our progress.

Clear the blockage - try to start afresh.

Not easy? - What is easy?

Nothing worth doing is going to be easy.

The mountain is steep and rocky. It has outcrops that bar our way. It has many a slippery surface. It has thorns and sharp grasses that cut and scrape our hands.

It has sharp rocks which stun and cut us to the quick. This mountain will be cold and sometimes dark. It will often make us want to turn back.
Each time we think of turning back, a resting place will appear. There may also appear a resting place when we do not realise that we need one. Perhaps we may have slogged and been so intent on our climb, that our reserves have to be replenished.

We sit on this ledge resting. We review our climb so far. What should we do? What should we not have done? Whose toes might we have trodden on in our haste? Whose peace might we have shattered in our eagerness to succeed?
Did we invade someone's privacy with our ruthlessness to succeed? For all these things we should ask forgiveness and the clearness of thought

not to keep doing the same things again and again. We should ask also, for patience with ourselves and others.

Being human, our patience may wear thin far too quickly, unlike our Unseen Friend, who is patience itself. When on our path, we should not be afraid to take note of whatever our Unseen Friend advises. We should not be embarrassed when the information is unusual and not the kind of thing colleagues are familiar with from us. We should stand up for ourselves more and ignore ridicule, even if it means asking for more strength from our Unseen Friend, yet again.

When on our way again the mists may arise. The clouds will often block our view, and we become perplexed. Who will we ask for help in the darkness?

We should ask our usual Friend. Some may ask 'Who is this Friend you call on for help?

The ones who know will answer.
The Friend Unseen, who follows all who venture up mountains.
The Friend Unseen who is there when we fall.
The Friend Unseen who knows our every mood, - our every fault, our every problem, our fear of being lost in the clouds.

He is there. He is there at our destination. He is there even if we do not reach our destination, for He knows that we have tried and climbed far, if not to the top.

COMRADES

The sky was dark, so very dark,
The sea was darker still,
He said he'd never forget that time,
I surely never will.

We'd tied down all the gear on deck,
And fastened all below,
We didn't then and never will,
Know where stray torpedoes go.

It's just our Great Creator,
Who knows whose number's up,
For who lasts through to see the dawn,
There is no winners cup.

Torpedoes on their dreadful course
Too late to turn the bow,
We knew so well what maimed before,
So what could happen now.

They hit us where we thought they would,
Right across the beam,
The noise so loud, the red and black cloud,
And the sound of the sailor's screams.

My mate said that I yelled so loud,
And it's still there in my head,
I opened my eyes, and I was alive,
For my comrades?, most were dead.

I march with my comrades in London,
Beside me, my sea-going friend,
A tear in the eye for each soul passing by
For the thousands who fought to the end.

CONFLICT II

Awoken from my reverie,
Aghast, I looked around,
I saw the hoards of people,
Strewn like rag dolls on the ground.

They lay there limp and lifeless
Bereft of living souls
Where once were lips and happy eyes
There now were blackened holes.

Mown down with no mercy,
Driven from their door,
Families, even little ones,
Plus many thousands more.

But, still the threats go on and on,
And, scenes of killing there,
The houses burnt right to the ground,
Till all the land lies bare.

I look round at my own small house,
Black walled and all forlorn,
This place where I was shot down dead,
Was the place where I was born.

COUNTDOWN

I'm often watching Countdown,
And my math's is getting better
My spelling is improving
By letter and by letter.

Often funny words appear,
Some are really strange,
Some letters are the dodgy kind
Impossible to arrange.

But, still, I like the challenge.
It keeps my brain cells on the move,
I kid myself I'm winning
But I'm merely in the groove.

CRAZY PAVING

When your heart's like crazy paving,
With the grass all showing through,
When you try to laugh, but life could be better,
And you don't know what to do.

Just shout for a friendly shoulder,
I've got two to spare,
Just let me know if you need my help,
And babe, I'll soon be there.

You may say "How can I know",
About the way that you may feel,
I know something of broken hearts,
Some things you can't conceal.

But,.....please don't feel embarrassed
If your thoughts you cannot share,
I simply thought it might be right,
To let you know I care.

CRYING OUT LOUD

Are these someone else's tears
That I am crying now?
Are they someone else's tears,
Because they know not how?
Is this someone else's grief
That I feel in my heart?
Is this someone else's pain
That pulls me right apart?
What can I do about it,
How ever much I care?
I think they're on the other side
I think there's someone there.
If there's someone out there
Please, tell me what to do?
Tell me who this person is,
Who's really missing you?

DAYBREAK

Lamps against the morning sky
Sky of pink and blue and grey,
Birds chirping in the trees,
They greet another day.

Colours changing every minute
Golden sun arising soon
Ever changing pinks and yellows,
Goodbye disappearing moon.

Slipping,- sliding - clouds of purple,
Touch horizon, one by one,
Fresh and bright with golden lining
Greet the rising morning sun.

DES'S DOUBLE

Des had brought two thoroughbreds
And they ran in lots of races
The other horses in contention
Just couldn't match the paces.

He raced them out at Chester
Then at Curragh too,
They ran the Oaks and Derby,
And Heavens, they just flew.

Then one season, where are they?
Had they fallen down a hole?
Des was happy for he knew,
That each had born a foal.

The first two they were super.
And each – a perfect mare
Now with foal adjoining,
This made it to four square.

Four square was a fitting name,
For this company of horses.
They gave him pride in every ride,
When scoring on the courses.

DESPAIR

It's when, what you really dread, simply happens
And your world comes tumbling down,
Family and friends start to gather,
They arrive from a far distant town.

The funeral comes, then is ended,
But your left with dregs of the past.
The one that you love has been taken,
To that heaven and homeland so vast.

It's bitter, you're hurting,- so painful,
But you knew that one day it would be.
You know that it happens on someday,
"But why must it happen to me?"

You know the answer already,
As all life must fit into place,
And, all of us part of that jigsaw,
Sometimes happy, sometimes sad, human race.

One day you will start to feel better,
Though now you are feeling so rough.
You find you just keep on crying,
And yes, how life can be tough.

Dev - Man with Horse Sense

Three cheers for Adrian Deverell
Or DEV, another title,
Or Little Crow - his Blackfoot name
To animals - He's vital................

Vital, because they need him,
An animals best friend,
St. Francis of Assisi
Would stand by him to the end.

Everywhere he wonders
He has a special way,
He gives that special care to them
On any single day.

He'll always spare a little time
For little cat or dog.
He'd do his best to save a life
Of goat or horse or hog.......

These people are so special
The ones who always give.
They make great contributions,
To the way the wildlife live............

DIANA, PRINCESS OF WALES.

Dear Diana, now at peace
With your special friend nearby,
No one in this world who cares
Could have a tearless eye.

We love you, dear Diana
Our prayers go out today.
You will be here in our hearts,
Forever come what may.

God bless you dear Diana,
God bless your special friend
God bless your driver also gone,
As on your way you wend.

After rest you'll bloom again,
But on the other side,
Once again you'll find your way
With the Master by your side.

We'll see a light around you
That light that shone within
You'll never die, you're in our hearts
A new world will begin.

DISAPPOINTMENT

Today's not any Saturday, for I've waited all the year.
But, sadly as life deals it, no the day is here;
I simply cannot make it, no matter what my wishes,
Even there's lots of things to eat set out on fancy dishes.
I'd see a bit of countryside and take a snap or two,
I go and get some healing which is what I'd hoped I'd do,
A day out with my other half are few and far between,
Except to wait in A&E, for that's the place we've been.
We need to see the countryside such as lean on farm yard gates!
But the thing that bothers me is I can't see all my mates.

DON'T BE AFRAID

"Don't be afraid", it said,
This notice on a bus.
Don't be afraid, I thought,
Not even make a fuss!

Maybe it was organized
For me to see just then.
I had simply walked outside,
Did someone else know when?

This message really struck a note,
For I'd felt so sick inside.
I'd had to take some drastic steps
That would cause a big divide.

Much too long I'd put it off,
This inevitable choice.
Now my monies almost gone,
Hark, was that the masters voice?

Yes, I think it was the voice
That guides us on our way.
The voice that calls us from the brink
Lest our strength should go astray.

I'd made my big decision,
And the wheels began to turn.
With help I've made a good fresh start
And someone had to learn.

It's sometimes sad in this big world,
With some things we have to do.
The way I'd suffered was unjust
And my messages were true.

Now I must remember
The words "Don't be afraid",
For I know the master loves us all
And he knows the choice I made

DOWN AND OUT

I've seen some places in my life, Where the day is full of strife.
I've met some folk - I'd rather leave behind,
On a tatty kind of beat that I hope I won't repeat,
Now I try to look for things far more refined.
They took me to the places that I never wished to be,
Met the gang that I never wished to know.
I met the kind of crowd, who were nasty, crude and loud,
And I told them, it was time for me to go.
They taunted me with meths and they showered stinking breaths,
They lay on beds that stank of beer and stuff.
They ate straight out of cans, brewed tea in moldy pans
And I never thought I'd feel so awful rough.
It's an awful rotten fate, if you're landed in that state,
It's enough to lose your wits and go insane.
It's not too nice to sit, drinking meths down in a pit,
And I never want to see the place again.
Now I'm finished with that street, and the gang I used to meet,
I've found my way and on the upward track,
I'll pray for them back there, with their ragged clothes and vacant stare,
And pray the Lord, will never send me back.
I thought that I had screamed, as I awoke, and I had dreamed,
Of a life I'd known, a long long time ago.
I'm so very glad it's passed and I'm completely clean at last,
I keep a notice to remind me that it's so.

EARLEY MORNING MIST

In the mist, I had surely missed her,
Galloping out in the morning dew.
Because of the mist, There was no vista.
She was missed and out of view.

She kicked up the sand on the nearby shoreline,
The mist slowly rose as she galloped along.
As she gathered speed it soon was a sure sign,
That she and the rider would not go wrong.

Then very soon, the sun was shining.
The mist all gone and the clouds all thin,
She'd gone out so fast, just like an arrow.
If she does it tomorrow, she may yet win.

How great it must be to gallop on the shoreline.
The rush of the air, sand and the sea,
The trust of the horse, the skill of the rider,
The thrill of the gallop, to be free, to be free.

The first light of the morning and off for a practise,
All saddled up and fresh as the sea.
Going off to the sand and the shoreline,
I can only imagine what a thrill it must be..

Easter Sunday Sunrise –
Bognor Regis 2010

I woke up early and stood at the window.
I saw the start of a brand new day.
The Sun shone bright and I thought of my good friends,
But, they couldn't see this scene, they were too far away.

I took some photos of this lovely dawning.
The red of the sun with the blue and the grey.
I'm glad I awoke on that early morning.
I'm glad that I stayed to watch the new day.

Many changes of the sky at sunrise,
Kept my attention as the sea changed too.
The sea was calm with the glow of sunrise,
As time passed that it gradually turned to blue.

It's good to wake up to see the lovely sunrise,
And I've often watched as the sun's gone down

(See cover picture)

EVERYWHERE

You are in the butterfly,
And maybe in the bee.
You are in the flower
And also in the tree.

You are in the sunshine,
You are in the hay,
You are in my deepest thoughts
At night and through the day.

You are in my living
And when the new dawn breaks,
One day I'll see you clearly
How ever long it takes.

Perhaps one day I'll see you
When standing on a hill
Among the trees and buttercups
And golden daffodils.

Sometimes when I'm really low
I picture your big smile.
Perhaps you'll come to see me,
Perhaps you'll stay awhile.

Life at times plays sudden tricks,
And deals the final card,
Even when I breathed my last
It never was so hard.

But then, I was sent right back again
To live and learn some more,
To live and say goodbye to you
As you pass through heaven's door.

FISHING BOATS

I sat on stones beside the wall,
And watched the fishing boats in the bay.
They rocked so gently on the waves,
'Til it was time to sail away.

Newly painted or freshly scrubbed,
They caught the glow of the fading sun.
The clouds were few and drifting off,
Leaving a bare sky, one by one.

The fisher men gathered on the harbour wall,
All getting set for the trip ahead.
While the rest in the pub order last rounds,
And the ones at home go off to bed.

The mast lights shine as the men go on board,
The lights shine on waves when they all set sail.
The scene has a blueness once the sun is gone,
Then the moon shines its face, all grey and pale.

FLU BUG

I'm listening to my ASPRO
As it fizzes in a cup
My mind is planning lots of things
But my body won't get up.

My eyes have gone all bloodshot
Like sets of traffic lights
I'm so dizzy I fall over,
When I'm pulling on my tights.

I'm sure there must be easier ways
Of getting one's self dressed
My blouse has now got crumpled up
Though once so neatly pressed.

Now, if I get myself quite steady,
I can put on my left shoe.
And just to feel more evened up
I'll try the right one too.

I get so angry with myself
When dressing takes too long
The 'flu can really drive you mad
When it makes you far from strong.

There surely MUST be easier ways
Of getting myself dressed
No matter when I try so hard
I end up so depressed

There must be some quite easy way
Of dealing with the 'flu.
So if you find some simple trick.
Then tell me, tell me do.........

FOOTLOOSE

I wish I could look from my window,
And see the green leaves on the trees,
If I could open the window myself,
I could feel the summertime breeze.

Just a short walk in the sunshine,
Would surely make the day sweet,
And I know I will do these things sometime,
As soon as I wear my new feet.

I'll walk down the road when I want to,
I'll even try riding a bike.
I'll remember and help those who saved me,
And allowed me to do things I like.

© Sylvia Blyth. 1998.

FOR ELFIE (ELFREDA)

Standing in a little shade,
Amid the stench and noise,
Was gathered close together
A group of girls and boys.

They watched the growing pile of shoes
Then clothes of girls and men,
There sat a man in uniform,
So busy with a pen.

As the names went in the book,
The tally grew much higher,
A people robbed of dignity
To end in shot or fire.

Gold was taken from their teeth
Dead bodies hit the ground,
Families had disappeared
Beneath a grimy mound.

26th for 27th January 2001
Holocaust Anniversary

FOXY

A fox crept past my window
One balmy night in June.
He thought he'd find some food outside,
Alas - he was too soon.

The bin men had a one day strike,
I guess they stayed in bed.
So no-one put their rubbish out,
The fox felt 'put out' instead.

More bad luck, the fox then found
When calling round next day.
His visit was the afternoon,
The bins were cleared away.

Soon he'll need something to eat
Or else he'll end up thin,
Don't be surprised if you look outside,
And see him in your bin.

Fred's Fancy

What a great jolly chap was our Fred,
That's a thing the whole country might have said.
Such an interesting man, there's no doubt.
He was good and tough, and was stout.
He knew such a lot about steam.
He liked a steam engine to gleam,
Old chimneys that stood in the town,
He'd watch as they pulled them all down.
Then later he'd add to his wealth,
By doing the job by himself.
And a steeplejack's quite a good job,
So he enjoyed earning quite a few bob.
He travelled in a van made of wood,
And he'd use the steam power when he could.
He'd help you out with a chore,
But, alas, Fred is with us no more.

Written on the death of Fred Dibner.

FREDA

A lovely lady, Freda,
Freda is our friend,
We've known her for a long, long time,
So this poem I have penned.

Freda lives in Essex,
A good few miles away,
But will be flying off quite soon,
For a U.S. Holiday.

We hope she will enjoy herself,
When family she meets,
We hope she has a lot of fun,
And lots and lots of treats.

We're wishing Freda Bon Voyage
When Whizzing off by plane,
We hope she will feel quite refreshed
When flying home again.

FREE SPIRIT

For months and months she lay there,
For months and months she cried,
No one really knew her pain,
In silence she had died.

Day by day she saw the sun
Slide across the wall,
Day by day she prayed for peace,
But peace was not for all.

Now up in a higher place
At peace and free to roam,
A free spirit, well remembered
And welcome in my home.

Many more have passed since then
Some have said Hello,
And I shall see them all again,
In the place where we all go.

Never ever far away,
Always near at hand,
The one who always knew my pain
The one to understand.

We spent so many many hours,
In perfect harmony,
And still again we're very close,
My super friend and me.

Perhaps a few could understand
Perhaps too few have cared,
But always I appreciate
The friendships that we shared.

FRIENDSHIP

Friendship is so special,
It grows there day by day,
It grows there daily bit by bit,
Like a summer's sunshine ray.

If nurtured there with kindness,
It grows to face the sun.
It blossoms like the lotus flower,
Complete when day is done.

24.9.98

FROM MBU TO YOU

I am twelve inches long, I'm a Mbu,
I'm a fish in a tank, - How do you do.

I'm quite a big chap, don't you think,
Too big to get washed down the sink.

I'm a colourful chap, some may say
A bit green, a bit brown, a bit grey.

I'm quite happy being a Mbu.
If I'm not, there's nowt I can do.

My cousin is a different coloured fellow,
He's grey and blue with some black and some yellow.

I have good size fins on my quarters,
It's good for when I swim in deep waters.

When I'm chased in waters so vast,
It's handy to swim VERY FAST.

That's my picture of me, a Mbu.
So goodnight and good luck, TOODLEOO.

GEORGE

He used to play the organ
At church on Sunday night,
Sometimes he'd practice early
And it always sounded right.

He'd play the music from way back,
Light hearted melody,
He put his heart and soul in it,
That was plain to see.

He also played the classics
And songs from old time shows,
He'd play them all so beautifully,
The list just grows and grows.

A special personality,
Was loved and still loved now.
I always loved to hear George play.
Step up George – Take your bow...

He'd come and play the hymns for us,
He'd make the organ sing,
THANK YOU for the way you were
THANKS FOR EVERYTHING.........

Sylvia B Blyth 1994

GOODBYE FOR NOW

I was not there when those brown eyes were closing.
But, I was there when they took her away.
She lay there covered except fot her face.
(You would think that she was sleeping.)
The vicar came in and he joined us to pray.

The service was good, I'm sure that it was,
The flowers were what she would love.
Friends and family were there in support,
Did she see us from her place above?

Not too often did words of anger
Pass those happy lips,
Even when the ignorant ones
Made their tasteless quips.

Many, many years have passed,
But, memories still are strong.
I've not met another like my Julia
As I've passed along.

HANDS OFF MY RELIGION

You may think I'm a joke, you can take a poke,
But I've had it with derision.
There are things with me you don't joke about
It's poking fun at my religion.

You can call me mad or call me sad
But I've made a firm decision,
I've got my life and church and friends
So hands off my religion.

If it's not your thing to pray and sing,
If it's just not in your vision,
Well, that's O.K, but I've had enough,
Don't tramp on my religion.

HEDGEHOGS DILEMMA

Does it seem like spring yet?
Have you looked outside?
The wind is cold, and where's the sun.
Don't open the door too wide.

I'm sure it should be springtime.
The foxes are about,
But, please you must be careful
And maybe not go out.

Look out again tomorrow to see if spring is here.
Some leaves are on the trees.
The sun came for just a while,
But, oh, that chilling breeze.

High Flyer or O.B.E.

I'm riding on my moped,
But I'm looking down on me.
I'm poised there-somewhere way on high,
Not where I ought to be.

It isn't very funny,
I must get back inside,
It's no good being way up here,
When going for a ride.

I'm heading for a corner,
And the traffic light.
AH! Thank goodness, here I am.
Now I'll be alright.

I'm back inside my body,
Before I had a fall,
Flying high and riding bikes,
Do not mix at all....................

(O.B.E.)Out of body experience.

HOME AGAIN

Kingston Ken is resting,
He's leaning against the tree.
He's a happy one when the day is done,
And he gazes out to the sea.

In London he'd sit by the window
And watch the folk go by.
But he missed his friends and family,
And he missed the seagull cry.

He missed the boats and the fishing.
And seeing the grandkids at play.
He missed the sun and its setting.
At the end of a long hot day.

He'd booked a flight to London,
'They said the streets were paved with gold'
He got a job that paid the rent,
But a lie he had been told.

Saving took him quite a while.
Enough for an aeroplane ride.
He'd done his work and did it well,
Next – homeward with his pride.

He was jolly there in London-
But, 'homesick' really won.
He needed his kin and the sandy shore,
And the calm of the setting sun.

It does no harm to wander,
To see 'what's o'er the hill',
Some folk wander round the world,
But, others never will.

NOT WAKE

If I should not wake up one day,
If I'm the first to go,
Remember all my love for you,
And, not all of it did show.
I'm sure I will not be afraid
When my new dawn breaks
It's just that I'll be missing you,
And the mode this dying takes.
Perhaps I'll go when sleeping,
And softly drift and sigh,
I'd like to dream of the life we'd had,
The sharing – you and I.
There's plenty in God's Heaven
I'll want to see some day.
'Til then, with family and friends,
On earth I'm pleased to stay.

IF ONLY

It's one of those "if only" days
When I've got you on my mind.
It's one of those frustrating days,
When I feel that I've been blind.

I didn't see the need just then
To say just what I thought.
I didn't see necessity
To rush with words I'd sought.

Now gone by a year and more,
And I've had time to think,
I see at last that my ideas
Have all gone down the sink.

If only I had realized,
How time goes by so fast.
I didn't know how long you'd stay.
How long your life would last.

I didn't want to think that way
The thought of losing you,
I didn't want to face the fact,
But now I'm having to.

"If only" is a simple phrase,
But really means so much.
I only hope and pray now
That we can keep in touch.

Jan - Jun

IN THE COLD LIGHT OF DAY

In the cold light of day
When you open your eyes,
The Sun may keep gleaming
From the blue of the skies.
But your mind keeps on turning
And it just won't stay still,
The Sun keeps on shining,
But to you there's a chill.

On the days when it's raining,
And the ground gets a drenching
Your brain is still turning
And your heart gets a wrenching
You remember the times
You both walked in the rain,
But this time alone,
You would walk out again.

IN THE GARDEN

I saw from my window the moon was so bright,
So I crept from my room to the garden last night.
I saw many creatures that roam in the dark,
I saw the two foxes that I saw in the park.
The eyes of the Owl beamed down from the tree,
For all I know they were looking at me.
But, really I think they were looking for mice,
A ready made supper, very nice, very nice.
A cat by the bush was seeking mice too,
But I doubt that he thought "one for me, one for you".
I went to my room with the moon on the wane,
Tomorrow I watch for the creatures again.

20.5. 2001

Is Love Indeed (28 Sept '06)

A little glance, a little smile,
A meerest chance to spend a while,
A chance to talk, and we would dream,
If we'd not met – what might have been.

Some time to share the things we love.
To grow as close as the hand in a glove,
To get to know each others need,
To share in all is love indeed.

When life is stressed we wait and fret,
We worry much, but not regret.
Our love was there so long ago.
Each others pain is sure to show.

All those years have gone so fast,
Our wedding vows are made at last.
A special ring – a wedding band,
I wear with pride on my left hand.

(Our Wedding day.)

IT'S GREAT TO FLY

I want to fly yet I tremble,
I shake, then nervously cough,
We drop into a pocket and wobble.
"Excuse me, the door just fell off".

"Don't worry", he said "You're O.K. there
You're nice and tightly strapped up".
"Oh yeah, I'm fine, but feel yukky,
Do you mind if I borrow that cup?".

"Just hang on and I'll close it"
Ah yes much better I think
Just one more photo, Ah! lovely,
"Excuse me, while I puke down the sink".

Of course, I'm joking it's lovely,
I'm often a bright shade of puce,
And I'm still saying fantastic,
As my head is stuck down the sluice.

© Sylvia B. Lloyd.

It's Great to Skate

Lovely, good to see you
To see you very nice, but,
Now it's not the ballroom
But dancing on the ice.

The music's very lively
The action lively too.
And gliding round the ice rink
Is what I love to do.

I am not a dancer,
Nor speeder, I confess,
But, I used to wear my skating boots
And my little skating dress.

It's good to see the costumes
So colourful and smart
The dancing all so lovely
And right there from the start.

With Holly there and Philip
To compere all the show.
It's got to be a lovely time,
So watch it and you'll know.

Flying round the ice rink,
Up there shoulder high,
It all looks so exciting
But, rather you than I.

I recall the dancing
Of Jane, and there with Chris.
Dancing to the Bolero
I'm glad I didn't miss.

They all do work so very hard.
It's a shame when one must go,
Then the winners stand to great applause,
With smiles all aglow.

Then week by week the numbers drop
The winners steal the show.
Week by week they learn some more,
It's skating, there they go.

Just a Small Problem

I feel so very, very small,
When I look up to the stars.
I know it's such a long, long way,
From Earth to get to Mars.

I feel so very, very small,
Compared to the Redwood Tree,
But, it never ever crossed my mind,
How tall I might yet be.

I still feel small, but not too small,
When standing by a bus.
But then, it would not make sense
If the bus was small,
It wouldn't hold all of us.

My Mother once said that I'd get big.
It takes some time and more,
Now I've grown up to six foot six,
A long way from three foot four.

KEDI, OH KEDI

Oh Kedi, how did you contain
So many years to just stay put,
So many thoughts and not complain
Then not to walk and not set foot?

Your years with family were spent,
With light and care, and doting love,
Not ever were you left alone,
Not even when drifting up above.

You were loved and are loved still,
In your home beyond the vale,
You lived your life the way you could,
Travelling on your bumpy trail.

On the passing of a friend's son.

LIFE WITHOUT LOVE

Two years without a cuddle
Two years without some love,
Who'd 've thought how lonely life could be
When new plans came from above.
Who'd think I'd go through bitter days
When life was truly Hell.
Who'd know that friends could understand,
The fear I knew so well.
Not knowing what the future holds
No-one to hold your hands,
Not seeing through some rose-tint glass,
At milk and honey lands.
But, then, one day you wake up.
Your cloud has left the sun,
You're suddenly on your road again,
And half the battle's won.
You get yourself together,
Do things you meant to do,
You start to plan your life again,
But from another view.
You find some new and better friend,
Than the one's from years before,
You simply open up your mind
To what there is in store.
You leave out all the promises,
For then there's none to break,
You just try hard to make things right.
With every step you take.
When safely on the road again,
And the road is straight and true,
You'll know you'll cope with knocks this time,
And your confidence see you through.

Life's Lessons

I have encountered on my road
So much that I would not have known.
These things I've learned or hope I have,
And many thoughts there, have been sown.

I make a wish, a sincere wish,
That, when I end this stay,
That I will have passed my utmost test,
Before I'm on my way.

And on my way to a fairer land,
Where we have been before.
And when I have been tutored enough down here
I'll be over there to learn some more.

Some mountains climbed have been so tough
But, they were meant to be,
A learning curve – I guess that's right,
A pure necessity.

Light and Love

We send you some light
For when the sun does not shine,
We'll pray for some hope,
When you search for a sign,
When the sun keeps on shining
But that's not enough,
We'll send all our love for you
When life gets too tough.

19.05 01

LOSING YOU

Perhaps one day I'll see you
When standing on a hill
Among the trees and buttercups
And golden daffodils.

Sometimes when I'm really low
I picture your big smile,
Perhaps you'll come to see me,
Perhaps you'll stay a while.

I know it's no use crying,
For now you're quite alright,
One day you may just walk on in,
All bathed in silver light.

It may be many years from now.
But I'm prepared to wait,
Then I'll be free to join you
Beyond the golden gate.

LOST AND FOUND

Life is not so happy
Since you went away,
I didn't know which way to turn,
I didn't know what to say.
I took a little time to think,
And get a note composed,
I thought I'd send you all my love
And your favourite picture enclosed.
I thought I'd go out for a walk
And I went out in the rain.
I started jumping puddles like we used to do,
But it could not be the same.
These memories keep flooding in,
Of the things you'd do and say.
I'd see your face so clearly,
Won't you please come back to stay?
I thought about the good times,
And all the sports we tried.
But nothing ever is the same,
Without you by my side.
I know that I must walk alone,
And, what must be must be,
But I'd tried to forget that you left this life,
In true reality.
Yet, to say that we are parted,
Simply is not true.
You only went to the Spirit World,
So I'll always be with you.
Now time has passed and I'm used to knowing
That you're with me in the rain.
I can now be happy,
And start my life again.

LOTS TO DO

Lots to do within the house,
And the garden's getting tall.
The garden gnomes have walked away
And the tortoise has climbed the wall.

The gate is there, well, I hope it is,
The last time that I looked.
The swing is swaying idly,
And partly is unhooked.

The chickens in the hen house,
Are looking rather shocked,
I saw in their eyes their big surprise,
Their hutch door was unlocked.

I let them out for an airing
For a moment out of doors
But, a shock I had on seeing,
The prints of fox's paws.

Quickly I re-cooped them,
For foxes love the chooks,
It's been written down for many years
And discovered by some cooks.

I really love the chickens,
I love the foxes too,
But the foxes love the chickens much too much.
Whatever can you do?.

I sorted all the problem
By mending all the fences.
It keeps the chickens safer
With not too many expenses.

There is but one who's losing out
And losing all his dinner.
The chickens all are getting fat,
The fox is getting thinner.

© Sylvia. B. Blyth.

LOVE'S FLAME

In the silent moments of the day
When that special one has gone away,
Remember that they've not gone far
Not even to the nearest star,
They'll be just there right by your side,
The gates of heaven open wide.
One day the moments of that day
Won't be so sad, and you can say,
They've gone away but there's no doubt
The flame of love is never out,
A toast to those just out of sight,
The flame of love is burning bright.

20.1.2002.

LUCIANO

I always love to listen,
As often as I can,
To a certain super Tenor,
A very special man.
I listen all attentive,
To hear that magical sound,
He has that certain something
That lifts you from the ground.
From every clear crescendo,
Of melody divine,
To sweeping through the octaves,
To low and rich and fine.
I cannot say too strongly,
The effect his singing gives,
I'm sure he will be always great,
For the peace within him lives.

4.10.95.

MALLEE ROOT

I bought a place at Salmon Gums with a lot of work, in sight
A lot of back ache and lots of sweat and working late at night.

We worked like hell to clear it, to make the land feel good,
We worked and scraped and burnt it, that bloody mallee wood.

Many years of working sheep and bringing up my stock.
Remembering the mallee wood I then had got a shock.

It was down at Albany with my brother and his wife,
Then I saw in a local shop something to help my life.

There were lots of items set around and all were made of wood,
I thought that if I'd known before how this would have been so good.

I'd burnt out all my mallee roots and never really thought
I could have used it then and there and people could have bought.

What a bloomin' waste it was, if only I had known
I'd dragged up all the mallee roots, instead had barley grown.

MAY FLOWERS

When I opened the door
It was past 2 a.m.
The night air was tinted with May.
The breeze in the trees
Brought a thought back to me
And I wished that you'd stayed one more day.

You just dropped by for a visit,
We both agreed not to make plans.
We neither were ready for what was in store
As the Gypsy read this from your hands.

She Said "Young man you were born to go roving
And you will go over the sea,"
But she didn't say when
You'd be home again,
Or if you'd be home back to me.

I waved to you from the doorway.
I stood there till you vanished from sight.
I stood there so long and looked at the moon.
With the May Flower scent in the night.

For months I waited and wondered,
I hoped for some message from you,
With no word and no sign.
That you were still mine.
I had to accept we were through.

Now it's many a long year since we parted,
Our union was not meant to be.
Then just one day more
And you stood at my door,
And you handed some May Flowers to me.

Midnight Vision

I was sailing at the dead of night
Upon the dark blue sea,
When all at once when the sea was calm
A vision came to me.

I saw a town all bathed in light
And a stable by an Inn,
A star was shining right above,
And a new child slept within.

The child was there, in swaddling clothes,
Asleep upon the hay,
The parents sat there full of pride
On that first Christmas Day.

9.12.97.

MISSING

I know that you are missing me,
Like you always do,
It was my time for moving on
As you will move on too.

You cried so much about me,
You cried both day and night,
But, don't be upset anymore,
As I'm really, Oh! So right.

Don't be upset about me,
I'm getting on quite well,
It's a lovely life on this side
There's so much I could tell.

Whenever you feel lonely,
Just think of what I've said.
I'll only be a thought away,
Don't fill your life with dread.

Tell them all, I'm O.K.,
I'm better than before,
I passed on through as you will too,
So you must fret no more.

Be happy for me, won't you
And know our love lives on?
It's helping me as I live here,
I'm not completely gone.

Morning Sun

The first rays of the sun are gleaming
The first shaft on the wall is streaming
And all across the garden beaming
And all the place is shining gold.

Making all of us feel better
Like the good news in a letter
Casting off the chains that fetter
Releasing many thoughts untold.

Shining on the birds and flowers.
Resting on the bush and bowers.
Sending warmth to last for hours
And nothing left is feeling cold.

Healing for the ones with illness.
Comfort for the humble homeless.
A calming in the summer stillness.
With all the warmth the world unfold.

MR ALFRED WAINWRIGHT

He loved to walk the rocky heights
And write for hours of glorious sights.
And dream and study through the nights
And talk of how the cold wind bites.

He'd take a bus then walk for hours
Whether in the sun or damping showers.
He'd go where the mighty Haystacks towers,
And walk amid the fields of flowers.

As time went on his sight had faded,
But in his mind no scene was jaded.
His walks on hills were now down graded
The facts of age had now pervaded.

His many books of Lakeland wanders
Are read and loved by they that ponders
And dream of mountains way out yonder
And know of nothing that he'd feel fonder.

MUM

Our Mother who will give her best
Who nursed us through our ills
Who served us needed medicines
Who checked on all our pills

Our Mother who has done her best
To help us through our tears,
The mum who sewed and clothed us
And cooked and cleaned for years.

Our Mother who did all she could
To help us on our way,
We thank you for the things you do,
On this your special day.

MY OLD DWELLING

There's a problem with my old dwelling,
The place that I was selling,
And the fact that my feet keep swelling
Means I just can't do these stairs there anymore.

The walls are really leaking
The boards are often creaking,
The mice are always squeaking.
The damp's got in and I cannot shut the door.

The back gardens gone to ruin,
It needs too much there, for doing,
The shed where I did my brewing
Is a pile of wood and I don't care anymore.

Maybe I'll buy a camper,
It maybe a little cramper
I'm sure it won't be damper.
And to be alone I'll simply shut the door.

NEED TO KNOW

When I was young and had to know
I asked so often but was not told
I waited so long with baited breath
Now I don't ask, I am too old.

You need to know the things you need
You need some knowledge about pain
You need to know to understand,
It's now too late to start again.

You need to know the ones to trust,
You need to know the reasons why,
You need to know why things go wrong,
To get things right before you die.

You need to find the ones to ask,
Is there a special kind of list?
A list of things that you must learn?
That no one told, so I had missed.

It could have saved a lot of time,
It would have saved a lot of stress
If told the things I'd asked about
The things that land you in a mess.

NELSON'S BRUSH UP

Nelson's got his top coat off
For all the world to see,
He's had a wash and brush up,
Now clean as clean can be.

They've taken down the scaffolding
They've replaced lots of stone,
They've cleaned his hat and scrubbed his face
It gives a better tone.

They've also scrubbed the wild beasts
Those lions around the statue,
It's a good thing that the lions are'nt live,
They might get up and grab you.

When they'd cleaned the Lions,
They filled in every crack,
And then they made them super smart,
With a coat of shiny black.

NESSIE OR NOT?

There cannot be a Nessie?
But, do we really know?
Have we plumbed the deepest depth,
As far as we can go?

Do we have an open mind,
To learn of something new?
Some have searched in a submarine
To see from a divers view.

Many strange big creatures
Are in the some far off sea.
So to see some kind of Nessie
Seems not too strange to me.

It may be up in Scotland,
It may be out in Spain.
I reckon dear old Nessie
Will lift its head again.

Night Fall

With frosty air at 2.00am
The snow began to fall,
It settled on the rugged tree,
It settled on the wall,

The wind blew up and made it swirl,
And it coated all the ledges,
It coated all the flower pots
And neatly sharpened hedges.

The snow was coating everything
Even corners of window panes
Sticking to cars in the junk yard,
Sticking to bars on the cranes.

All was quiet and peaceful,
In the morning as I put on my socks,
Then I saw with surprise, on the pathway
The foot prints of the fox.

When the town is asleep in the night time,
It must be the best time to call,
But, as everything was shifted the night before,
The fox had nothing at all.

In the daytime I looked from my window,
The traffic was there but still,
Really I like to go shopping,
It's not urgent, so I don't think I will.

The news men say you should stay in,
Particularly the elderly or sick.
So I'll stay by the fire and heed the news,
As the snow fall is much too thick.

Sometimes there are things that you might do,
And some that you simply leave out.
There days when you can do nothing at all,
And things you can do nothing about.

NIGHT OUT

He was feeling rather weary and creeping back to bed,
And feeling that the ceiling was rushing to his head.

The walls were getting closer he feared they'll squash him thin.
The dustcart's coming round today there's going to be a din.

His brain was turning cartwheels and the sky was much too bright,
And Oh! He wished he hadn't had that extra gin last night.

NOW AND ALWAYS

I'd hug you in these wanting arms,
These arms and heart that have loved
You since your birth
And loving now, when I cannot hug
Since you've left this earth.

You did your time of schooling,
You served your work time too.
You spent the time to send out love,
But, naturally, that's you.

You showed that you could understand,
Many sick ones like yourself,
I'm sure you showed many in your way
There were multi kinds of wealth.

Wealth in you was simple,
And simple you are not,
You came along and touched us all,
With all the love you've got.

© Sylvia Blyth 1st June 2014 and these verses
are for Julia for the 21st year since her moving on.

ODE TO HALLOWEEN

With Greying whiskers and shawn head,
He warms the pillow on his bed.
And starts to dream at dead of night.
But, does not snuff out any light.

He dreams of wizards, phantoms too,
Black cats and witches fill his view.
Then cats and witches start to chase,
But, he cannot find a hiding place.

He runs and runs within his dream.
The cats all howl, the witches scream.
They keep on running close behind,
Running wild - right through his mind.

He tosses and turns in his small bed,
But cannot get them from his head.
Never slowing always there,
The ever faithful night time fare.

Then, as daylight filters through,
The shadows change a shape or two.
Too soon alas, goodnight the sun,
Another night times round begun.

He does not want to fall asleep,
And hear the trees all groan and creak,
But eyes now close with endless strain,
The witches scream within his brain.

Now within the nightmare grasp.
The howls, the screams, the screeches rasp.
But before he goes insane,
The morning light comes back again.

10.10.95.

ON ROOFTOPS AND PLANT POTS

On rooftops and plant pots
With snow so sparkling white,
Sparkling white in the daytime,
Sparkling blue at night.

Twinkling on the branches
Where fluffed up birds are sat,
Twinkling on the porch outside,
And on the frozen mat.

Freezing toes and fingers,
Freezing for dogs paws,
It all looks very pretty,
But, I think I'll stay indoors.

© Jan 2011

ON THE EDGE OF MORNING

On the edge of Morning
Clouds reflect the sun
Letting in the tiniest light,
To show the day's begun.

The birds begin to twitter,
And wake up in the trees,
The leaves fall off and flutter down
They dance in Autumn's breeze.

You hear the bottles rattle,
On the milk float down the street,
As foxes bark as they go home,
With their usual hunting treat!

19.05.01

ON YOUR WAY

If reaching out is hard to do,
And reach right out you must.
Find someone to help you soon
Find someone to trust.

Someone else may help you
In sorting out the snag.
Sitting worried on your own
Will always be a drag.

Don't wait too long in seeking,
Seek out the ones that know.
Seek out the ones who've been there,
Then on your way you go.................

OUR CORNER OF HEAVEN

There's a house down there on the corner
It waits there for me and for you,
There's a sky and a lake and it's for us to take,
And He painted it all over in blue.

There are clouds up there in the Heavens,
He painted them silver, white and grey.
For we need rain clouds for the flowers
As they brighten up any old day.

There's an arch, by the house, in the garden
It's covered in leaves all so green.
Between the leaves are the flowers,
A prettier sight never seen.

There are cats and dogs in the garden,
There are fish in the lake - wait and see.
The fish that we lost at great personal cost,
And they'll wait there for you and for me.

19.10.1997

OUR MATE BILL

There's not too many people
Reach the age of our pal Bill,
There's some who are not half the gent
For that's some job to fill.

He's such a lovely feller
And I'm sure you'll all agree
That he deserves the best we've got,
Be it Tizer, Scotch or Tea.

It's the first time that I've met you Bill,
And, of course, that you will know
But, with Jim and friends who call on you,
You'll see how friendships grow.

12.8.2001.

Pained and Strained

How strained, how pained, how difficult,
When in a family feud.
How sensitive, what a strain to live,
When outside hurts intrude.
How hard it is to get away,
And find a little peace,
And then, when you are on your own,
Find your tension won't release.
Oh! What a combination,
Of family strife and calm,
Reach out and grasp a friendly hand,
Accept a soothing balm.
I know these complications,
They stab you in the heart,
It churns up all emotions,
Than pulls them all apart.
If only I could know the way,
To soothe the troubled mind.
To help you find serenity,
And leave the hates behind.

PAM'S CHOOKS

Pam's been plagued by foxes
They took some chooks away,
Instead of foxes in the night
They robbed her in the day.

I hear they didn't take the lot,
I think she's now got ten,
But now the chooks are right fed up
Being shut up in the pen.

Pam wanted them for free range,
That was the whole intention,
For chickens safe and foxes out,
May need a new invention.

The chooks should be out on the grass
It makes for better laying
But it's just no good if they're all locked up
And the fox is out there playing.

PATCH

Patch, he was a lively dog,
With Shandy on the run,
They chased the trains along the fence
And had a lot of fun.

The drivers in the trains they chased
Would hoot as they went by,
The dogs would bark excitedly,
Not catch up, but they'd try.

He liked to play with road cones,
He'd keep one if I let him,
So I let him play with an old car tyre,
Just to 'not upset him'.

Sometimes he'd see a football,
When the boys played on the green,
If they threw the ball he'd head it,
It's the best trick that we've seen.

All of this was years ago,
But memories linger on.
I hope they have fun like they used to do
In the place where they have gone.

PAUL'S CHICKENS

Paul had bought some chickens,
He kept them in the yard,
To round them up at bedtime,
He finds it very hard.

The first six they were easy,
They were a dosey lot,
He warned them he'd get nasty
Watch out for the cooking pot.

The next six they were tricky
they raced around the pound,
When chasing them Paul slipped and fell
Ending full length on the ground.

Paul got up and staggered,
With mud from head to toe,
"I'll get you chickens in" he said,
"Right now, so in you go".

PAUL'S CHOOKS

Off they go, and running
Charging round the field,
They all had got the exercise
But it didn't help the yield.

By twelve o'clock he'd caught them,
And all were in the pen,
At least he thought he'd got them all,
But, where's the oldest hen?

He hunted round the garden
The kitchen garden to.
Then he found a hidden nest
With eggs, quite a few.

Out came the strutting chicken,
From bushes by the wall,
He put the chicken with her mates,
So glad he'd found them all.

He took the eggs that chicky laid,
And put them in the store,
Know then that some time soon,
She would lay some more.

PEN AND PAD

September, October, November Oh my!
How the time goes flying on by.
What a good time I had,
With my pen and my pad,
And thought what a glad soul am I.

I had spent some long hours,
'Neath the trees, by the flowers,
And made use of my pad
And the pen that I had,
Then walked home in occasional showers.

I had to use my grey matter,
When the verse seemed much flatter
Then my pen would crumble,
And the sky start to rumble,
And on my pad the rains pitter patter.

PENGUIN SPEAKS

Look out for the Golden Eagle
He shows his wings so fine,
He holds them up and out so wide,
Not a bit like mine!!

Look out for the little Robin,
His chest is oh so pink,
My old chest is flat and wide,
And rather dull I think.

Eagle and Robin speak

It doesn't matter what they think,
Or how they look at you,
You are a good smart Penguin,
So you is simply YOU.

12.12.2002.

POEMS AND RHYMES

I was asked how I get all my poems,
Well, I guess ways are new all the time.
I find all the facts and the details,
Then I make them make sense and to rhyme.

Sometimes I will alter the rhythm,
If that is what's needed and then,
I make sure the story's still working,
And keep on that rhythm again.

© Sylvia. B. Blyth. 5.6.01.

PRECIPITATION

"Some precipitation in the weather!"
By the weather girl, we'd been told.
What it means, I don't know,
But it's simply freezing cold.

It's blowing round my ankles,
It's freezing round my head,
If that's precipitation,
I think I'll stay in bed.

We know it's cold in winter,
That's what it is about,
But, it's trotting about in a dressing gown,
And never going out.

It's cancelling my nights out,
Never seeing friends.
It's getting puffy ankles
And my knee joint when it bends

And Oh! This freezing weather,
Can't wait until it ends.

Quantum Physics

It's all to do with Physics
The moment that we die.
It's the moment of our way of life
On earth for you and I.

It can seem complicated.
But it's just the way things are.
You cannot kill the energy
That keeps us here, thus far.

We die and find an altered state,
Our souls will carry on
However we depart this world,
Our souls are never gone.

Our very soul and spirit,
Will be till God says when.
So we must progress all we can
And serve our God till then.

May 2006

Rainbow Garden

Red for tulips and for roses,
Green for leaves in little poses
Lemon gladioli neat,
Dark green moss beneath your feet.
Blue delphinium by the wall,
Yellow sunflower, wide and tall,
Pink carnation, light green stalk,
White for lilies where you walk.
Purple lavender and blue,
Lilac bushes tint the view,
Dark pink antirrhinum there,
Silver leaf and maiden hair.
Light green cactus by the house,
Light brown fur on harvest mouse,
Gold and orange marigold,
Salmon pink for lilies bold.
All these colours for your garden,
If one left out, I beg your pardon.

September 1994

REALISATION

When I stepped out of the train I saw the splendid view,
I took up my luggage and knew just what to do.
I walked towards the mountain and the great big rocky face.
A little wonder round and there I found the place.

I climbed the rocky mountain and nearly reached the sky,
Up among the birds, so silent as they fly.
When looking out around me I saw the English Plain,
Then all at once, I shuddered, and shook, and shook again.

Then I had awoken in a bed and in a ward,
A nurse said "if in pain", I should, "simply pull the chord".
I wanted to get up but, I could go nowhere.
In this small room was just a bed and chair.

I lay there in the quiet then heard a violin,
The air was warm enough, but seemed so very thin.
I tried to hear the music but it would simply fade away.
I didn't know where I was or what was the time of day.

I looked towards the picture but it slid right down the wall
I tried to look about me then, there was nothing there at all,
I tried to call out loud, but no words came from my mouth,
I didn't know which way up I was, looking north or south.

A disconnected voice said that I'd "had a nasty fall"
I felt that I was slipping and I remembered the mountain wall,
And that was many months ago when I awoke in bed,
I couldn't find a reason so I thought that I was dead.

After a while, I learnt to walk on a couple of pegs.
Soon I shall be walking on a brand new pair of legs.

REALLY

Crass exaggeration, that's what I see today.
They may not think they say it, but it happens come what may.

They say they like to sunbathe and end up nearly black.
She said "a little exercise", and nearly broke her back.

They said they'd buy a little food and bought up half the shop.
And then they took a month of leave and nearly got the chop.

He said he wasn't really sad as he shed a little tear,
But when you look a second time he's crying in his beer.

Maybe I am simple, maybe I am hard,
But it makes me sad when they say one inch, then walk off with one yard.

Crass exaggeration can sometimes be quite daft.
He promised you a schooner, - "but, what a lovely raft".

One day they went out fishing to get the biggest fish of all,
Then they placed it on a tea plate, and it looked so very small.

There was a man in Wales who'd boast "ten thousand sheep",
But the wool he got from all that lot was quite a tiny heap.

They said "we'll mend the pick-up, it only takes a while",
But the time it took to fix it, they could lift it half a mile.

There must be a hundred thousand exaggerations every day,
I could think of lots and lots, well, a dozen anyway!

15.7.96.

(Crass - Grossly stupid, without sensibility)

REMEMBERING

The guns just went on bursting
The shells would find their mark,
The bullets went on screaming,
Making hellfire in the dark.

The Sailors, Soldiers and Airmen
Made ready at each post,
Not knowing on the morrow,
Which unit hit the most.

But still the rain kept pouring,
Making puddles in the trench.
One Soldier went delirious
He could not stand the stench.

With no way to push on forward
And no word to draw back,
The only thing a soul can do
Is stay right on the track.

The walls were wet and slimy,
The ditch a river bed,
The slimy walls and the injured calls
And the smell of the helpless dead.

A flare went up from the enemy
And lit up all the site.
The flare lit up the site like a horror film,
That went on night by night.

But then the guns got dimmer,
As mist began to fall
Apart from a cry from the souls that die,
There was no sound at all.

Three days later word came through,
The war was at its end,
Now to count the mortal loss,
Of brother, sister, friend.

The seventh day of silence,
And far from trench and mud
But still recalled within the mind,
The stench, the noise, the thud.

The screeching now abated,
The guns and tanks in rows,
The sounds of peace as the bombings cease
Is what the Soldier knows.

© September 1996.

Ripples

Toss a little pebble
See it plop into the lake.
And see the many ripples
A pebble thrown can make.

The ripples would go wider,
If the water had been flat.
Then, the water calms right down
Till it's smooth just like a mat.

I sat down in my kitchen.
With music and my books
And I looked out to the dark grey sky,
And I worried at how it looks.

The room had been so quiet,
Even tranquil, I could say,
But, then a mighty crashing
Took all the peace away.

The crashing was so sudden
And the the sudden rain,
It poured down like a waterfall
That overloads the drain.

After days of raining
With gulleys filling up
There was no water for drinking
Not near to fill a cup.

The water kept on rising,
We left our home by boat.
The water was just everywhere,
Our house had got a moat.

The water got to everyone.
Stretching wide and like a lake,
The boat that saved us from the flood,
Left ripples in its wake.

Now I am much older, and
Still walk down to the lake.
I toss a little stone or two
Just for old times sake.

I remembered all the ripples
In the lake so long ago.
I stood and sighed and watched the tide,
And I'd write down all I know.

RISEN

Our paper had gone with a sudden crash,
But now has risen as though from ash.
Now it has started its life a new,
Just like our human spirits do.
We missed our special paper indeed,
It meets our special spiritual need.
Though the old one now is gone,
Like spirits rise our paper lives on.
I thank the people there concerned
And see a tribute you have earned.
So don't be downhearted we're doing well,
And remember the name of Barbanell.

On the demise and rise of the Psychic News.

ROBIN

Looking from my window
On a cold, cold snowy day,
I saw a robin on a post,
I heard the robin say.

I'm cold out here and hungry too,
Can I have some dinner,
Some sustenance is what I need
Or I'll be getting thinner?

Yes indeed, my little friend,
Your dinner's coming up,
Your drink is sparkling water
In case you wish to sup.

The little robin ate the food,
He drank the water too,
He bowed and scraped so humbly,
"I thank you - Toodle loo!!"

RUNAWAY

I existed over there
To keep two souls afloat,
I fought through ills and terror,
And, escape did seem remote.

I had to keep on hoping
and keep on keeping on
For if I failed and got dragged down
All my hope was gone.

I had to strive for better days,
And another place to live.
I couldn't stay there any more
Without a thing to give.

The love that was had long run out.
While fighting so much hate.
I had to salvage what I could,
To flee and close a gate.

If I hadn't run away
God knows where I'd be.
I had to help another soul,
So I took my child with me.

I couldn't last another year,
My wits were ebbing fast.
I made a choice and took a chance,
And now there's peace at last.

As I look back through the years,
There was no other way.
I had to make another start,
And live another day.

We make mistakes, we often do,
But, then you have to go
I never asked for half the grief
How much, you'll never know.

19.5.95.

SAD LAND

I went outside to think a while
My heart was beating wild,
My thoughts went out to the children there,
My God, to every child.

Just left to figure out this world,
To starve and be alone,
Stripped of love from family,
And dumped - like bags of stone.

Not a decent thing to wear
Not a single toy,
Just two nasty smelly cots
For this little girl and boy.

I saw these things on news time,
It really makes you weep,
I thought when in my nice clean bed,
How do these babies sleep?

Maybe, from sheer exhaustion,
From crying all the day.
Why must this keep on happening,
Is there no other way?

We carry on with all our prayers,
And, carry on we must,
For even now another soul
May be left out on the dust.

Later, when the fuss dies down,
"It's just another story."
A news man got his front page stuff,
And bathes in short term glory.

But, that's not where the story ends,
The mindful will be saying,
The ones there working will keep on,
The rest will keep on praying.

Some doing every menial task,
With lots of love thrown in,
They're healing in their own sweet way,
That's where it will begin.

If and when those tots survive,
Whoever gets to live,
I wonder who will first explain
And teach them to forgive?

1991

SCHMOOBOO

Schmooboo was our hamster,
And she had her little house.
I heard her rustle in her bed,
As quiet as a mouse..

She had a see-through plastic ball,
And we called it her car.
She loved to toddle round in it,
If let, she'd toddle far.

Schubert Franz Peter Schubert
31 Jan 1797 – 19 Nov 1828

I found a friend the other day,
Which really stirred my heart
The music stayed within my mind
And Schubert played his part.

The music played, the people sang,
They calmed my weary day.
I'll play the music more and more
To chase my blues away.

Away and away, and out of sight,
And let my body mend.
Let the music heal my soul.
Let the sad days end.

SEAFARING ODE

With all stocked below I said 'off we go'
And we left Swanage Quay very nicely.

With the log book spread out, and my bread and my stout,
I wrote in my log quite precisely.

Then with log stowed away on that bright sunny day,
I looked to the journey before me.

I said my goodbyes – and noticed no cries,
It was clear that they did not adore me.

SEEN FROM MY HIDING PLACE

Shells are falling round about,
The walls are caving in
There are tanks on fire and people too
And what a hellish din.

The sun's blocked out by thick black smoke
The school has blown sky high.
The road is full of craters,
No place for you and I.

People run off to a hut,
Their clothes are torn to shreds.
Bloodstains on their shoeless feet,
And bloodstains on their heads.

They're looking for a first aid camp,
But not one can be found.
Yesterday the air-raid struck
And bombed the whole camp down.

The air is thick and sickly,
With cordite and the dust.
There are bodies rotting in the cars,
Along with mud and rust.

It all looks such an awful sight,
With buildings blown away.
No living person now in sight.
No reason left to stay.

If only heads of state and such
Would make peace over all,
Then there would not be the deaths
Of folk against the wall.

2.4.95.

Shadow on the Wall

I've felt so sad since you first went
And that I'll never laugh again,
My memories of you go round and round,
And it's the strangest steady pain.

Sometimes I feel you're near me,
Like a shadow on the wall,
I want to reach out and touch you,
But I can't see you at all.

Sometimes I hold your jumper,
The one that mother made.
The colour there may go in time,
But my love will never fade.

Days will pass and months will pass,
And years will mount up too,
Then I will pass from this great world
And I will look for you.

SHAKY

I feel so very, very tired
My eyes keep closing up
I'd like to take a cup of tea,
But I cannot lift the cup.

My hands do seem so shaky
My knees are shaking too.
I think I'll have to go to sleep,
So I'll say Goodnight to you.

SHANDY

Shandy was a lovely dog
A coat as soft as silk,
A temperament of a perfect gent,
No other met his ilk.

He'd act so lordly out on runs,
But still would walk my pace,
His lovely eyes and gentleness,
And what a lovely face.

He'd play and bark with Patchy
His pal from years gone by,
But now they've gone, the doggie pals,
To the kennel in the sky.

SHE'S FAST ASLEEP

"She's fast asleep", the father said
As he closed the bedroom door.

And fast asleep she surely was
But there was much much more.

Her father reached the lowest stair
And to his surprise,

There she stood in golden light,
Right before his eyes.

He stood and watched with puzzled gaze,
The child he'd seen in bed.

Then gradually the vision went
And not a word was said.

A moment later back upstairs,
His mind still in a whirl.

He looked and saw astounded -
There was his little girl.

She looked asleep, she really did.
It could not be denied.

But when he checked the child again
He found that she had died.

She came to see them often,
Just as they hoped she would.

She came there softly all in light
Just where she once had stood.

14.7.2001.

SHETLAND WRECK

All the men were lifted off,
The craft had dipped one side.
The gulls flew ever near the deck,
With each progressing tide.

The vessel drifted near the coast,
With a fierce cold gale blowing
It drifted much too near the rocks,
As many fears were growing.

Many a storm cloud building up,
The cold bit to the core.
As the vessel drifted further still
Up to the Shetland shore.

People stood and watched for hours,
They stood and watched in vain.
As the vessel sank and rolled about,
Amid the oil stain.

The beaches now a slimy mess
With clumps of shiny black.
The bodies of so many birds
Collected in a sack.

Then lots of birds in lots of sacks,
So many died in pain.
So many in the Shetland Isles
Will never fly again.

The tanker sunk and broken up,
Each section rolling free.
The oil a lasting nature threat,
Up in the Northern Sea.

Sleep Walk

Round and round the garden
With rollers in her hair
Round and round the garden
And, how the neighbors stare.

Looking under hedgerows
Trots across the lawn,
Treading on the frosty grass
Just before the dawn.

Searching with the torch light
Scrabbling in the shed.
Up the road and back again
Then back into bed.

SOME CHILDREN

Some children born are perfect,
Some children are in pain.
Some children don't stay very long,
And they fly home again.

My child had some problems,
In fact she just survived,
Her heart had stopped at one week old
With help she was revived.

Julia walked at six years old,
Where as many walk at one.
Considering her problems
It's great what she had done.

Julia went to junior school,
Then into seniors too,
And later into working life,
The way that most folk do.

One day she was sitting still,
At the start of another day,
But then an angel called on her
And took my girl away.

Though it's many years now,
Since Julia went away,
I can't explain how emptiness
Can get to me each day.

SOME DOGS

Dogs can be workers but sometimes they're real tearjerkers,
Or you get laughs 'til aching in both sides.
If you're sick, they're right there with you,
Or at night they'll stay and guard you,
And for you they would hold back the tides.

The days I got to know them though it seems so long ago,
They were caring and they got right to my heart,
But as the time passed by they got old like you and I,
Now their absence just tears me right apart.

Something

Something here is happening
You're here, but no longer here.
You start an emotion in my heart,
Of partly lost love and fear.

You cannot love me any more.
I know it's no one's error.
But, to know the love that we once shared.
It's gone, and now I feel a terror.

A simple feeling, I'd not known,
Since events did break my heart,
Events so unexpected
And now I feel apart.

Though you are here and I am here,
Each in a separate world,
What a strange and lonely outcome,
Has this event unfurled.

SPRING BACK

The trees held back for many weeks,
The weather far too cold.
Then suddenly it seemed to me
The leaves were out and bold.

The winter weeks were cold enough,
Thick snow around the land,
Now and then a glimpse of sun,
Then frost to heart and hand.

Welcome to a later spring,
With flowers all in bloom,
Uplifting colours and perfume now,
For garden, park and room.

SUFFOLK PUNCH

He stands so tall and pulls a cart,
A chest so wide and strong
A coat that's smooth and shiny
He works the whole day long.

He has a mane that's flowing
Or plaited for the shows.
He has a mighty power
Evereywhere he goes.,

You hear his hooves clip-clopping
About the countryside.
Doing his work for the farmer,
The Suffolk Punch has pride.

T.E. and The Helper

You'll know him in the summertime,
Or with the autumn breeze.
You'll recognize that special help
When you tremble at the knees.

He'll be there on your happy days,
Or when you're feeling low.
He'll speak with you in slumber hours,
As you will surely know.

You'll get to know him better
With every visit made,
And maybe, all these years apart,
Will somehow be repaid.

6.5.87.

TEARS

Empty out your sadness
Let it flow away
Let your tears flow freely
As on a rainy day

When emptied you'll feel better
For tears may clog the soul
Now look ahead and face the world
For once more you are whole

TELEPHONE

There's a thing in our house called a phone,
A plastic machine – dog and bone,
You can love it or hate it for sure,
It'll ring as you've walked out the door,
If you wait, it won't ring anymore.
You can try to find out who had wrung,
You can ask 'till you wear out your tongue.
You can hunt 'till you nearly turn green.
It's the phone, that rotten machine.
Who ever – they never ring back,
Was it John was it Sheila or Jack?
I would ask if I ever had a chance,
But no number was left in advance.
I think I might just send out notes
Before they all come in white coats.
I might yet go raving mad,
Or simply sit down – very sad.
Not knowing who rang is a pain,
Ring ring ring – There goes that machine once again.
I push all the buttons they ask.
I'm sure that they talk through a mask.
They ask why I phoned them at all,
And I tell them they made the call.
I put down the phone and I think
Much more and they'll drive me to drink.
If you want me to know when you call
There's a machine – and it's just down the hall,
It is handy to know who's down the line,
I'd be grateful for just one small sign.
If you can't do that I can't win,
I shall shove the machine in the bin.
Of course it's a daft thing to do,
But, if you were me, wouldn't you?

TELL ME

Tell me, if I should hug you too tight,
If I should love you too much,
When you bid me goodnight?

Tell me, if I should miss just one sign
Maybe, I miss when you call,
But always know you are mine?

Tell me, when each day finds its end,
You'll be by my side.
For on you I depend.

When it's the end of our time,
When we leave our own place
Can I still say you're mine?

Tell me?

TEMPUS FUGIT

Seven years or seven days,
I miss her in so many ways.
Some days those eyes of hers just shone
Then life in those brown eyes was gone.
One moment know that she is there,
Her grandma stands to comb her hair.
The usual things to do each morning,
But, then was gone without a warning.
From here within I tell you truly,
My heart still aches for my girl Julie.

5.6.01.

THE CHOIR SANG

Tons of stone and glass and wood,
Upon a plain, the massive building stood.
At the end of a journey, the vision took place,
Just a trek on a cycle, never a race.

The trek was started miles away,
Early April on a warm and sunny day.

Some towns and some villages, some quite tiny,
Trees that dwarfed houses, leafy or spiney.

Passing through farmland with fields of corn and maize,
Bringing back memories of school holidays.

Getting on to evening and nearly at the end,
I saw the massive building when riding round the bend.

The sun was low, near setting, a crimson orb it seemed,
It shone onto the windows which instantly gleamed.

At the very top of the building a large cross stood bold,
The sun shone bright on the building and the cross was shimmering
gold.

Daffodils swayed gently in the breeze outside, candles burned brightly
within,
I had no reason to rush off home and the service was about to begin.

When the choir sang in the soft candle light, you would think you had
drifted above,
With good people around and the heavenly sound, the place was
surrounded with love.

© Sylvia Blyth - Easter 2013

THE CROSS

Now with special cross in place,
See the smile upon his face.
The time is gone when roof was bare,
But still inside our God was there.
Our God lives there within the walls,
He is there when the needy calls.
He'll be there when in your pain,
When in your peace, He's there again.
We welcome him with all his grace,
The light will flow from his dear face.
May the light shine evermore,
And shine with peace on every door.

20. 1. 2002

The Cross on our church was blown down in a gale,
This poem was to mark its replacement.

THE FALLING LADY

Right at the rostrum the Medium stood,
She leant on the bar of polished wood.
She spoke of a room spinning round and round
And of a lady falling to the ground.

The lady she had seen was very still,
And by appearances was very ill.
The Medium was drawn to a lady in the hall,
"You know this lady who has had a fall?"

The lady said "you're right, and she was very old,
At least, that's the story I was told".
The medium said no, no, this was today,
Go and find out, help her, be on your way".

The lady got up and left the place,
In great speed as if in a race.
She contacted her friends and family for sure,
To find the sick person and get to her door.

The lady was located and phone calls made
Many who knew her rushed to her aid.
The lady who fell stayed a long time friend,
With a hospital stay she was soon on the mend.

THE HEDGEHOG

Lively little hedgehog,
With back so sharp and spiny,
Funny little turned up nose,
And eyes so brown and shiny.

Strong but dainty little feet
That plod along the ground,
That scrape among the grass and hedge,
And spread the leaves around.

When the summer's finished
He looks for food to keep
To hide away for wintertime,
And his hibernation sleep.

Little grunts and sniffing
When looking for his lunch,
Finding nuts and berries
To crack and crunch and munch......

THE OAK

Tall strong Oak Tree,
With branches thick and wide,
When someone chops your branches off,
What do you feel inside?

You cannot run and hide somewhere,
You cannot hide your face.
Sometimes you grow another branch,
But you never slip from grace.

Big tall Oak Tree,
When leaves are brown or green,
You show to me great strength in life,
If power can be seen.

Tall strong Oak Tree,
We could learn from you.
We could find our strength again,
In everything we do.

The Other Side or N.D.E.

I breathed my last short breath of air,
And it cut me like a knife.
I jumped a simple barrier,
Which marks both death and life.

Like an express train I travelled,
Speeding through the night.
On unseen rails in a starlit sky,
And heading for the light.

Some time, some place along the way,
I said to someone near,
"I have two children there at home
I cannot stay up here".

The light had got much brighter
Then, at some point went away.
I woke up in the hospital,
To live another day.

Some people don't believe me,
When I speak of my ordeal.
To me it really happened
And I know it's real.

THE SANCTUARY

What a lovely time on Saturday!
On our visit down to Shere.
Meeting yu with friends and laughing too,
At Harry Edwards home of cheer.

We had our turn of healing,
We had a dinner too,
And a walk down to the cherry trees,
And saw a marvellous view.

What a lovely house it is
All is so refined,
The people looking after us,
All are very kind.

I must go back and visit
And spend some lovely hours,
See the healing Sanctuary
And see the lovely flowers.

THE TIME AWAY - JULIA

A time away – the very last.
The holiday before she passed.
A time away from usual places
But, someone there to tie her laces.

A happy soul with friendly ways,
Had helped her well for many days.
She could not know what would befall
We could not tell, - not know at all.

Julia went in quiet peace,
A quick retreat, a quick release,
In quickness too, our sudden pain,
Julia's loss made tears like rain.

Tears will tumble as they did,
Some were seen, though others hid.
I know I'll see her later on,
But, what a gap since she has gone.

Remembering: Betty Nye, her helper on holiday.

THE WEDDING DAY

On the morning I awoke, wondering immensely,
Looking at the early sky, studying it intensely,
But, yet, knowing all the while
He'd have great reason for a smile.

A smile to last eternity, a look to mean so much to me,
A joining of two hearts forever, a feeling that, this God is clever.
Making us to feel this way, and not knowing half what to say.

Not long to wait, a short few hours of mind wondering, and tense feet
shifting.
A time of knowing that two hearts are one,
That part of life over - over and done.
Tender hearts knowing they're won, tenderer even, the spirits heavenly
lifting.

Now finally the moment faced, where hands are joined, and rings are placed.
All necessary words "now repeat", then formality complete,
Now stress that mounted falls away, they've reached their very special day

Then quietly, as each takes a seat,
Two sets of loving eyes, they meet.
Glorious sunshine in the skies,
Great depths of fulfillment in their eyes.

Happiness, bursting from every pore,
Happiness, reaching to the very core,
Eager to start their life together.
And ready to see what's in life's store.

Cameras clicking all around, shifting feet on grassy ground,
Picture the pair with glowing faces,
Knowing the pair are going places,
Not bothering with airs and graces.

Thingy Halloween 2

Way down at the witchy pool,
When most are fast asleep,
A thingy, that's without a name,
Will then begin to creep.

It creeps among the willow trees,
It stirs the sleeping mice,
It loves to frighten little bats,
And, that isn't very nice.

It trundles through the fungi patch,
Knocking off their heads,
It makes a dash across the field,
And ruins turnip beds.

And then, at last, the garden gate,
Oh dear, it's traveled far,
It scampers along the princes path,
And hides down in the jar.

There's lots of room for a thingy there,
In a jar so big and wide,
So watch out if you pass that way,
Could be, a thingy is there inside.

31.10.2000

THINKING A LITTLE DEEPER

Isn't life strange?

Unexpected happenings along life's way can change ones way of thinking. This is particularly true when the thing that 'wakes you up', so to speak, is nearer to home or of your own home life. This has happened to me on several occasions where I had been trundling on, doing my own thing, then, crash-bang, someone becomes very ill or has died.

Of course things do happen as we grow up. Alas, we don't take time right then to qualify or make sense of things. Many things are put on the back burner for various reasons.

Unless a family is quite lucky, there are usually accidents or bouts of 'flu etc.

The thing that happened that affected my family was when I gave birth to a child with a handicap. Julia was born with Spina Bifida and Hydro Cephalous and didn't walk until she was six.

My daughter arriving with her extra needs was a turning point and a special mark in the calendar.

I began to see life with new eyes. Very likely, even neighbour's thoughts were influenced when they knew of her problems. Of course, unless neighbours are asked, we don't know their thoughts.

Out of nowhere and quickly we all needed to be aware of her fragility and care that was so important for this tiny being among us.

Right from the start her standard of life was in question or if she would cope at all. As she was born by Caesarean Section I did not see her until she was 2 weeks old having been moved from St Helier Hospital to Westminster Hospital the morning after birth. My daughter did live.

She not only lived, she taught many to think deeper about others less able than ourselves.

Julia was bright, she was not academic but was not to be fooled either. Julia was kind.

She would buy presents for our birthdays and Christmas, or have someone shop for her.

Her wrapping of a present was something else. Friends at her Church called her the Sellotape Queen. She remembered others well.

On more that one occasion she helped raise charity funds. Before Julia died, prior to Christmas 1993, all her presents for family and friends, were wrapped and ready.

On the 21st she died at the age of 31, from a blood clot on the lung.

This year, is the 10th anniversary of her passing. We've all had time to reflect on the difference Julia made to our lives.

When I see people with a handicap now, I can honestly say that my thoughts go much deeper than before Julia was with us.

At no time can I recall her to say "Why am I like this"? or "Why can't I be like other people"?

She did not complain. I can spend hours on meditating on all the good things Julia gave us.

20.9.03

THOUGHTS AFTER A PASSING

A day we know that had to come,
Try as we might to keep it at bay
A pain that strikes you at the heart,
A pain that will not go away.

That day has gone and all feel numb,
Then thoughts go round and round your head,
You recall those chatty days
The words you thought but never said.

But never fear of words unsaid,
Some words unsaid will often keep,
And later, when you feel more calm,
Your words may travel in your sleep.

Your words may travel to were they're meant,
The words that stayed within your brain,
They'll fade away like melting snow,
And you will be at peace again.

In memory of HRH Elizabeth Queen Mother.

8.4.2002

TOMATO FROG

To change from a frog to tomato,
Is extraordinarily strange,
I've seen film clips of age old tricks
But none of them quite in that range.
I love to eat firm red tomatoes,
And I doubt that they'd ever been frogs
But just to make sure that those tricks are no more,
I'll chase old frogs back to the bogs.

© 18.4.1997

TWIN TOWERS

I awoke with good intentions
To do things I needed to do,
I awoke with good intentions, yes,
To a nightmare that was true.

I awoke with good intentions
But, something got in the way
Once I'd turned the TV on,
It was an awful day.

It showed some people rushing
It showed great clouds of dust,
I watched a lot of helpers
Doing what they must.

A lot of people covered
In dust as white as snow,
Struggling to get a breath - the rest-
You wouldn't want to know!!

Smoke and dust that suffocates,
Leaves people on the ground,
Cars and shops demolished,
Chaos all around.

It started with an aero plane
It aimed right at the tower.
And then the other tower was struck
Within one half an hour.

What an awful tragedy,
And see it all unfold,.
I'm sure I'll think of all of it
When I am very old.

Lots of people on that day
Can't live to age at all,
The crime against humanity
Is written on the wall.

I don't remember in my life,
Seeing such a state,
First one and then the other -
The Towers - disintegrate.

I'd lit a candle earlier,
When seeing what went on,
Knowing physically you just can't help,
And knowing lives are gone.

14. 9. 01

WAR OF THE WAVES

The waves were getting wilder
The storm was getting rough.
The water in my bath was cold
Life can be quite tough.

I rescued my command boat,
Dry docked my submarine.
I rescued all the soldiers
Now all nicely clean.

I found the bar of bath soap,
All so yucky now.
I jumped out from that mucky sea
And gave a little bow.

I'd done a really splendid job,
I'd won my little war.
Tomorrow I will tame the sea
And bath a little more.

WAR

Another land, another war,
Another reason dying for.
Another leader filled with hate,
Thousands meet an awful fate.

One man with a power strong,
Enough to drag a state along.
Enough to do his bidding there,
For people's souls, he does not care.

The leader stands there oh so smart,
Uniformed to play the part,
A smile to show the world he's sweet,
And mocking dead men at his feet.

He'll stand there looking oh so snug,
Like preying mantis with a bug.
He'll stand and say things just to psych,
Then like the mantis he will strike.

Little boys still fresh from school
Thin and hungry, made a fool,
Made to fight and cut to pieces,
A thousand souls the war releases.

White Noise E.V.P. Electronic Voice Phenomenon

I was listening to the radio,
Between the stations too,
I paused there at the white noise,
When a voice I knew came through.

For a moment I was shocked
With some exclamation,
To voice of any kind
When not on any station.

I tried and tried and tried again,
To find where I had found the voice.
Then suddenly in another place;
"You see, you have another choice."

"You see it is not just one place
Where you can find our voices,
You just find the patience
For a myriad of choices."

© Sylvia.B.Blyth 6.Nov 2012

WHITER THAN WHITE

Whiter than white as the icy wind blows.
The oversized flakes of lace like snows.
Landing in the gullies where the yellow gorse grows,
And melting into water where the mountain stream flows.

Whiter than white it lands on leafless trees,
Floating into valleys on a light calm breeze.
Landing on outcrops and high cliff ledges,
Catching in the branches of close cut hedges.

Swirling in high drifts in seldom used lanes,
Whiter than white on the steep hill and the plains.
All bright and twinkling when the sun shines on the heather.
Even something beautiful in freezing weather.

Landing on ice on the paddling pool.
Topping like a hat on the dainty toadstool.
Landing on the bars of the old school gate
And the children play snowballs and get home late.

© Sylvia Blyth - Easter 2012

Printed in Great Britain
by Amazon